OUT OF THE LIFESTYLE INTO THE ARMS OF JESUS

An Ex-Lesbian's Journey

Michelle X. Smith

To My Dear Sweet, Beautiful friend!! Michelle Love you

PRODIGAL PURSUED

Out of the Lifestyle Into the Arms of Jesus—An Ex-Lesbian's Journey

Printed in the USA

Library of Congress Control Number: 2016937930

ISBN (Print): 978-0-9974667-0-6 | ISBN (Kindle): 978-0-9974667-1-3

Some names and identifying details have been changed to protect the privacy of individuals.

To Contact the Author:

WWW.PRODIGALPURSUED.COM
WWW.MICHELLEXSMITH.COM

What Others Are Saying

Michelle, a mortally wounded woman, receives a miraculous transformation. Her memoir is raw and vivid, an exposé of explicit sexual and occult activities that totally captured Michelle's life for many years. The story unfolds, revealing the true love of a long-suffering and compassionate man who would not let her go, no matter how far and fast she ran. Also on stage with Michelle are family and friends who eventually become heroes for their divine determination.

—Hal Linhardt
Director, Kansas City Evangelist's Fellowship
Missionary with IHOPKC

Prodigal Pursued inspires me to never quit believing in what God can do in the life of a lost or wandering soul. Michelle's book is honest, real, and uncondemningly convincing in its truth. The truth of it demands a response—pressing deeper into the heart and holiness of Jesus Christ, or be left pondering the inescapable truths presented. Reading it will leave you more excited than ever about praying for and reaching the lost, wandering, and confused souls Jesus Christ loves so much. I am left amazed at the love of Jesus Christ that is ever wooing the sons and daughters of Adam into deeper relationship with Him.

—Mike Stubbs
Senior Pastor, Victory Fellowship
Emporia, KS

Poignant. Clear. Real. These are just a few of the words I would use to describe *Prodigal Pursued.* As a pastor I have been across the desk from many who have journeyed through the struggle of same-sex attraction. In fact, I know the struggle all too well. The way Michelle shares her story gets right to the heart of the matter without pulling any punches and at the same time release love into a topic that is avoided by many in the church. Kudos Michelle—may your book meet the prodigal right where they're at—in the place of being pursued by their Father.

—JACOB BISWELL
Senior Pastor, Living Word Worship Center
www.jacobbiswell.com

Prodigal Pursued offers transparent words from the heart of a woman made brave by the power of God's love. She reveals the secret struggle behind reconciling an open choice with a conflicted heart. Michelle's authenticity and vulnerability are beautifully expressed through the pages. You won't be able to read it without connecting emotionally. Her story will challenge you to wrap Truth in Love and share it with the world.

—WENDY K. WALTERS
Life Strategist, Motivational Speaker, Author
www.wendykwalters.com

Acknowledgements

Although I would like to acknowledge and thank everyone who helped me on this journey and name each one individually, I am sure to inadvertently leave someone out. That would make me sad and I would want to add a sticker to every single book with that person's name. Then I would realize I left someone else's name off the list and I'd have to get another sticker. You can see where this would lead, but there are some standouts I have to mention.

- To the prayer warriors of Victory Fellowship Church, the Friday Morning Fire Corps, my Book Team, and Bonnie Ott. Ott, thank you for all the prayers and support.
- This book is dedicated to my sister, friend, and mentor, Donna Blanchard. She never stopped believing and praying that I would come back.
- A special and heartfelt debt of gratitude to my mom and dad. They never stopped praying for me.

Prayer is truly powerful.

Contents

Prologue

I was an out, loud, and proud lesbian for almost 25 years. I was a feminist, a separatist, and an anarchist. I believed in sex and a lot of it, creating pools of intimacy with many other women. Before that I was a child who loved Jesus more than anything—I fought my way out of intimacy with Jesus to pursue what the world offered. I went from New Age beliefs to witchcraft to Buddhism to agnosticism and back again. I changed my attitudes and beliefs only slightly less regularly than I changed my shirt and slightly more frequently than the changing of the seasons.

I'm writing this book not because I think I have something new to share, but because I care about you—the lesbian, the "gay Christian," the homosexual. God has placed a burden in my heart for other people who are where I was, people who are sweet and funny, caustic and wry, clever and heartbroken. You might not believe you have been snared, entrapped, bewitched, or drawn, but you have been. I hope my story will shine light into your circumstances. I pray God will use the opened veins of my journey to illuminate your path back to Him.

I'm also writing to other Christians who want to know more about this people group. I'm writing to you, believers who care about people who are sexually broken. You are the Christians who desire to understand how to have tough conversations in love. For too long the church has erred on the side of truth—preaching condemnation without any acknowledgement of the Father's love for all. Then the pendulum swung and now many churches and believers are preaching only love—a love without requirement, without a need for obedience or fidelity.

The Bible is clear that truth and love are braided together. We must hear, believe, and tell about the Father's Love which will anchor the requirements of Truth.

CHAPTER 1

Small Town Childhood

PICTURE GOD NUDGING YOU AND ME AWAKE BEFORE DAWN BECAUSE HE CAN HARDLY WAIT TO BE WITH US.

–BETH MOORE

CHILDLIKE FAITH

I was adopted. The parents I knew had come for me a few short days after I was born. The summer of 1967 my biological mother, Sarah[1], was a brand new high school graduate, working as a waitress when she met my biological father. He was a traveling magazine salesman in Toledo, Ohio and met Sarah at the restaurant. They were together for the week he was in town.

The only person Sarah confided in that she was pregnant was her sister-in-law from California. As the time for my arrival approached, she boarded a train bound for her sister's house. Her plan was to give birth there, give me up for adoption, then return home. However, in the middle of the country, she went in to labor. A nurse on the train informed the conductor the train would need to stop in the next town which had a hospital.

The unscheduled stop just happened to be Emporia, Kansas. They put Sarah in a cab and she arrived at the hospital in the middle of the night. I was born a few hours later. Before they gave her pain medication, she told the doctor her plan to give her baby up for adoption. The doctor on call had met with a couple a week or so before and told them they were infertile. The young couple was still fresh in his mind when Sarah said she didn't want to keep her baby.

Their names were Carl and Marletta Smith. They didn't have a phone, so the doctor's nurse spent a couple of days trying to reach Marletta's parents. They had a phone, but it was a party line. Finally she got through and was eventually able to speak directly to Carl and Marletta. They decided, sight unseen, they wanted me. It was an hour's drive to the hospital and while they were gone to pick me up, my grandpa and a young uncle put together a crib for me.

I don't have any memory of living without a deep awareness of God. My mom says she led me in a simple prayer to accept Him "into my heart" when I was just two and a half. I fell in love with Jesus as a little girl.

Fast forward to age five and the summer days stretched endlessly before me. The trailer where we lived was filled with sunlight. I was waiting for the dew on the grass to dry so I could run outside to play. The green carpet was clean and fresh. I had been playing with toys on the floor, but as I played, I thought about Jesus. The night before we had watched a Billy Graham crusade on television and I realized I wanted Jesus to live inside me.

I got up and looked around, but no one was there. I knew I needed to kneel in order to do this important thing. The cedar chest my dad had refurbished sat near the green, gold, and brown couch. I knelt down in front of the chest, folded my hands, bent my head, and asked Jesus, "to live in my heart forever." I felt happy I would have Jesus as my friend and that He would always be with me.

I lived in Virgil with my adoptive parents. Virgil was a rural Kansas town with a population of 102, of which I was related to a good many. However, there were no other kids my age until I was in second grade. The McKenzie's moved to town when I was seven and two of the four boys were close to my age. They were heavily involved in the family farm and 4-H though, so I still didn't have a constant companion. Starting when I was about seven or eight, I would go on long exploratory walks or bike rides in the countryside. All the roads were dirt and gravel, except where they were overgrown with grass and weeds. I loved traveling down those roads by myself, talking to Jesus.

Three months before my ninth birthday, my parents gave a little boy a new home and adopted my brother. It was the day after Thanksgiving. I was in the living room watching Santa's Workshop when the phone rang. Mom got off the phone and told me my baby brother had been born. Dad, mom, and I drove two hours to pick up the tiny newborn the next day.

Virgil, population 102 (now 103), had a grocery store, filling station, post office, the co-op, and a beer joint. There was one church in town, a Methodist one. We attended church and Sunday school every week. I enjoyed going, but what I loved most of all was Bible study on Tuesday mornings.

SUMMER CAMP

There had once been a high school in town, but around the time I was born it was closed. The Baptists purchased the grounds, including the three-story school building and gymnasium. They converted it into a summer church camp and put Rev. Locke in charge. He came to town on Tuesday mornings to meet with a small group of women and lead a Bible study. I would sit at the table, listening, and asking questions. Sometimes, I would pretend to be sick so I didn't have to go to school on Tuesday mornings in hopes Mom would still take me with her to the Bible study.

Rev. Locke was an older man, full of laughter and love. He lived his life according to the Bible. He picked up hitchhikers because he believed they might be angels—if they weren't, it was a chance to tell someone about Jesus' love. He visited men in jails, held little children on his knee, and prayed over groups of teenagers. Even though he wasn't young and hip, teens and children alike loved him. His church camp was popular in large part because of him.

Because Rev. Locke knew me and my parents (and probably more importantly because I begged as only seven- and eight-year-old girls can) he allowed me to go to summer camp before I was technically old enough to attend.

Rev. Locke looked at me with his kind, blue eyes.

"I suppose Michelle can come to the three-day camp this year."

I jumped up and squealed, yanking on my mom's arm.

Mom hushed me.

"If she gets homesick, she can just walk down the hill and be home," he said.

I knew I wasn't going to be anything so weak as homesick, but I didn't say anything. I didn't want to risk him changing his mind.

I not only didn't get homesick, I got "camp sick" whenever camp wasn't up and running. It didn't matter what group was attending, I wanted to be there too. The only time I was strictly banned was when it was an all boys' session. At camp, I was fortunate to meet several foreign missionaries. I knew early in life I was called to go to the mission field. I assumed it would be somewhere in Africa, or maybe Mexico. I believed I would be a missionary, meet my future husband on the mission field, and get married under an oak tree surrounded by wildflowers. We would eventually move back to the United States to pastor a church.

BIBLICAL FOUNDATIONS

I also loved Billy Graham crusades. Whenever I knew Billy Graham was going to be on, I couldn't wait until dinner was over so I could go get the television warmed up. I watched from the first song to the last refrain of "Just as I Am." An avid and precocious reader, I devoured books like *The Hiding Place, The Late, Great Planet Earth, Joni, The Screwtape Letters, The Cross and the Switchblade, Run, Baby,*

Run, Satan is Alive and *Well on Planet Earth.* I read every Spire Christian and The Crusaders comic I could lay my hands on, and many of the Jack Chick tracts. I also read *Amityville Horror, Louis L'Amour*, *Sherlock Holmes*, Agatha Christie novels, the encyclopedia, and basically any book that came within arm's reach.

The Cross and the Switchblade had a particular impact on me. It is the story of Nicky Cruz as told by Rev. David Wilkerson. Nicky was a tough gang leader in New York City and Rev. Wilkerson was a pastor from Pennsylvania called by God to minister in the toughest neighborhoods in New York. In the book, I read about the baptism of the Holy Spirit with the evidence of speaking in tongues for the first time. I was nine or ten years old and the churches we attended did not endorse such a thing, but I knew I wanted it. I knelt in front of the green striped love seat where I'd been reading and prayed to have this baptism. I had no idea what "speaking in tongues" might sound like and wouldn't until we began attending a Pentecostal church when I was 14.

In spite of all the strong biblical foundation, I had a vein of rebellion running through my being. I was stubborn, intractable, and curious. I loved "experiences." I wanted to experience everything, feel everything—especially the pleasurable. I was a hedonist at heart. Early on, I believed with every experience, I gained value. Unfortunately, I did not believe I already had value. I was told (often in a demeaning tone of voice) that all I had was "book smarts." From this criticism I concluded the only way

IN SPITE OF ALL THE STRONG BIBLICAL FOUNDATION, I HAD A VEIN OF REBELLION RUNNING THROUGH MY BEING.

my thoughts and opinions could ever have true value was if I could pair my intellect with experiences.

Mom and Dad

My mom was 18 when I was born and my dad was 24. Mom swept the kitchen floor after every meal and mopped every day after breakfast. Her house was immaculate 24 hours a day, seven days a week. When I was assigned a housekeeping task, I was expected to reach the same level as mom did. Her sister, my aunt Jan, would joke years later about coming to visit and my mom getting up to clean the ashtray every time my aunt would tap her ash off the cigarette.

Dad was a hard worker who loved his family. He could fix anything from a toaster to a roof. He worked for the school district, which encompassed several small towns, but the schools were located in Madison, 20 miles from Virgil. He drove the school bus, worked as the elementary school custodian, and in the evenings drove the bus again, which delivered athletes home after practice. If there were evening activities or games in the gym, he worked those as well. His jobs had him working from 6:30 a.m. to 9 or 10 p.m. many nights. He also worked a half day on Saturdays.

Mom was young and stubborn. I was precocious and headstrong pretty much from the womb. To say we butted heads would be an understatement. Mom wanted to raise me correctly, to teach me all the lessons she thought I needed to learn. Her life was focused on religion and rules. I wanted to rebel and have experiences (perhaps just to experience rebellion). I was sensitive and took every correction as a gash to my soul. Mom wanted to toughen me for the world. I thrive on affirmation, words of acknowledgement, but harsh or unfair criticism bruised my soul and threatened to break my spirit. I learned to seek out what I needed from other adults.

Grief and Sadness

"Michelle, sit down," Mom patted the table. Dad sat to her left.

I sat down. I knew this couldn't be good. The last time they'd sat me at the table like this was when they told me I was adopted.

"Your Aunt Jan has cancer," mom said quietly, measuring my response.

Eleven years older than me, Aunt Jan was the epitome of cool and I adored her with every fiber of my being. The blow was enormous.

Within a month, I was back at the kitchen table again.

"Michelle," mom began, "I'm going to have to take your dad to Wichita to see an eye specialist. His diabetes is causing his retinas to bleed."

"What next?" I thought.

We went to visit my aunt's family while she was in the hospital having her lymph nodes and spleen removed. When we returned home from this sad trip, I discovered my dog had died.

The more sorrow I experienced, the more painfully aware I became that I was not popular or athletically gifted. I didn't think I was cute or pretty. Boys didn't get crushes on me like they did on some of the other girls. No one was ever heartsick over me. I felt alone.

One day, a young woman from church (whom I greatly admired) declared her lesbianism. I was 14 at the time and she was a freshman in college. It made an impact.

I heard some of the other girls in junior high saying I was gay. Looking back from an adult's perspective, I see this was just a common way to insult someone who was a tomboy. If I'd been a girly-girl, the rumor might have been that I was a slut. As I wasn't into hair, make-up, or frilly clothes, "gay" was the insult of choice. I know now that words have power and I can accept or reject words said about me. I didn't understand that back then.

TOMBOYS HAVE FEELINGS TOO

I was a tomboy my entire life. My mom made me wear pretty dresses when I was little, but got frustrated I wouldn't act like a little lady while wearing them. I would end up showing my panties or the dress and tights would be grass-stained and torn. Eventually she gave up and let me wear blue jeans. I know this bothered her and she would frequently comment on how I dressed or how I moved. She thought I walked like a boy and made her displeasure known.

Mom didn't want me to wear makeup until I was 14 or 16, but by then, all of my peers had been experimenting with cosmetics since they were 10 or 11 years old. I was embarrassed to go through a learning stage so long after witnessing their early attempts. To this day, I have probably not worn makeup more than a dozen times.

This criticism of my appearance, even though I also heard compliments, led me to feel like I was "less than" the other females.

All of these events are knotted together in a viscous morass of guilt, pain, sadness, and loneliness. Even looking back 30 years later, I still want to curl up in a dark hole and cry. Nothing about my world made sense or felt safe and comfortable.

Between my freshman and sophomore years in high school, we moved to Madison, which is where I'd been going to school since I was in kindergarten. I played sports, I had a part-time job in a small restaurant. I attended Campus Life, a Youth for Christ high school ministry. When I was a junior, David and Donna Blanchard, a young, on fire couple, took over as the new leaders of the ministry. I immediately felt a strong kinship with Donna and she became like my big sister.

They took a group of youth to Mexico for a month-long mission trip and my childhood curiosity for missions awakened into passion. When David and Donna made plans to move to a Texas border town in order to be full-time missionaries to Mexico, I started imagining myself moving there as soon as I graduated from high school.

ENDNOTE:

1. Sarah is not my biological mother's real name. Some names and identifying details have been changed throughout this manuscript to protect the privacy of individuals.

CHAPTER 2

The Chasm Begins

Pornography is to sex what McDonalds is to food. A plasticized, generic version of the real thing.

—GAIL DINES

DISCOVERING PORNOGRAPHY

I was young, certainly younger than seven, when a boy a few years older introduced me to "dirty magazines." Pictures of naked women, provocative poses, spread legs, and seductive expressions of desire, need, and want were laid before me. In hindsight, I'm pretty sure these were *Hustler* magazines, far more hardcore than *Playboy*. We were in a "clubhouse," which was really just a ramshackle wooden shed not used for anything any more.

We sat on something like old mattresses or sofa cushions. I remember being in this clubhouse more than once and with different kids. One time we played a game of passing our fingers through a lit candle flame. The clubhouse was dark, with thin rays of sunshine pushing through empty knotholes and vertical cracks in the walls. It was dusty and hot, so whenever someone came in or out of the clubhouse, a welcome cool, sweet breeze would blow through. Otherwise, it was still inside. It smelled of dust, oil, and chickens.

Porn was more difficult to find back in the days before the internet and cable. Still, I wanted to find more. I wanted to see those pictures again, but I also knew it was wrong. I couldn't just ask an older kid to show me, I had to wait. When I was a few years older I started babysitting and discovered many men kept porn magazines in their homes, readily discoverable once the kids were in bed. One man kept tall stacks behind his recliner in the living room.

The magazines other than *Playboy* featured picture layouts of two women, as well as stories of lesbian sex. Those magazines didn't feature naked men, only naked women, and at seven to 12 years of age, men were still foreign, strange, unknown, and dangerous.[1]

When my mom went grocery shopping, I would go stand by the paperback books and read while I waited for her to finish. I would just grab a book at random and flip to a page in the middle and start reading. I quickly discovered the dirty parts, thinly veiled to blatantly obvious sex scenes. During these weekly grocery shopping expeditions, I became adept at finding the books most likely to have those steamy sections. Even in the 1980s, some of these scenes involved two women.

I had discovered masturbation by accident when I was a child. When I was four or five years old, I climbed a pole. The stimulation brought on a distinct pleasure I instinctively and immediately knew must be kept completely secret. I sought ways to re-create the sensation and soon developed a habit. By the time I was in high school, it was a frequent habit. As a young adult, it became a nightly addiction. The grocery store reading fed my fantasies which in turn fueled this habit.

FLASHBACKS

I have had frightening flashes of memories going back to my early childhood of being handled by an adult male. One of the clearest is of a man's hand clamped over my mouth, pressing down, and the hairs on the back of his hand are rubbing against my nose. The feeling is one of being pinned down, unable to breathe, and nausea.

Another is of a man's eyes looking in a rearview mirror at me and I'm filled with dread. I believe when I was very young, perhaps between three and six, something untoward happened.

I can't say more because I just don't remember. Although I don't remember any other specifics, I know these experiences changed how I saw myself as a girl and subsequently how I viewed men. As a teenager and into adulthood I thought of men as being other, alien, and dangerous.

QUESTIONING

By the time I was fourteen, I was questioning why God would say women couldn't be with women. This sounds similar to Satan's ploy with Eve in the garden. "Surely God didn't actually say that?"[2] By age seventeen I had a huge secret. I was openly rebelling against my parents and God by thinking of myself as equally interested in both males and females.

I lived a secret life in my head, engaged in my own fantasies. I assured myself I would never act on these, but even then I knew better. At the time, what I believed in every fiber of my being was no one I knew from the church—no Christian—could be trusted with my secret. They would hate me. They would tell me I was evil. They would tell me I was going to hell. This was the mid-1980s and to my knowledge, the church at large did not have a developed theology for people struggling with homosexuality. In fact, I remember hearing the newly discovered AIDS virus was a punishment from God because the "wages of sin is death."[3]

I LIVED A SECRET LIFE IN MY HEAD, ENGAGED IN MY OWN FANTASIES.

I believed I was going to hell because I had feelings of attraction for other females. This belief gave me a sick, anxious feeling in my gut constantly. By the time I graduated high school I could no longer stand myself or these feelings, and I figured if I was going to hell anyway, I might as well act on my feelings.

DATING BOYS

I only dated three boys when I was between the ages of fourteen and eighteen. Not for lack of interest on my part, but because I wasn't ever chosen by any boys. I didn't go on dates because I wasn't asked out. I assumed—no, I knew—I wasn't someone boys were interested in. By the time I got to the last boyfriend, I mentally thought of myself as bisexual.

The afternoon before what was to be our last date, I read a *Cosmo* magazine article in the school library about giving your boyfriend oral sex. It appeared this was something straight girls did and, at least according this article and the numerous pornographic vignettes I'd read, they enjoyed doing it. It was something new to experience.

That night we parked in the lot by the swimming pool and started our usual kissing and fondling. I was feeling powerful, full of seduction, and I took it to the next level. I unzipped his pants and started performing oral sex on him. Unfortunately, it turned out not to be all the magazine had said it would be. I found it tiring and completely unsatisfying. He attempted to digitally bring me to climax, but it was even more tiring and unsatisfying.

This failure of a first sexual experience convinced me I was not bisexual, but an all-out lesbian. I thought if I was sexually aroused by males, this experience would have been satisfying. I gave him back his class ring when he dropped me off at home and I ran inside. I was crying. I told Mom we'd broken up, but not why. I tried to call Donna, my friend and youth minister. When I couldn't reach her, I just collapsed on my bed and surrendered. Literally, I surrendered myself to the identity I was sure was mine.

WHO AM I?

At this point, I had been struggling with my identity for five or six years. Who was I? Why didn't boys like me? Why wasn't I like the other girls? Why was I so different? I had been struggling for even longer with my secret nighttime compulsive addiction.

My parents and church leaders had all taught me these things were wrong. I had been raised to believe masturbation, sexual fantasy, pornography, bisexuality, lesbianism, and premarital sex were all sinful. I believed they were all sinful. I wasn't in doubt. I wasn't on the fence. I didn't think these activities were open to interpretation or debate. I tried to stop, to give it up, but I was hooked.

During these years I continued attending church, loving Jesus, serving God, praising God, going to youth group, and reading my Bible. The one thing I didn't do was tell anyone, not one single soul, about my issues or struggles. My pride and fear were too big. I had thought about telling Donna, but I couldn't get past the shame and embarrassment. At some point, my emotions solidified into defiance. Defiance is a much easier emotion to deal with than shame.

Surrendered to My Fate

That night, I just gave up. I continued attending church, but I felt like a hypocrite. I began to drink more alcohol. I started smoking cigarettes on a more regular basis.

The summer after I graduated from high school I gravitated towards people I knew from neighboring high schools who were a year or two older than me. I had heard they were lesbians. They took me to my first gay bar. I went back the next night and got picked up for the first time. I followed her back to her place and had sex with a woman for the first time. She was experienced sexually and it was far more emotionally and physically satisfying than it had been with my boyfriend. This time was filled with everything I had been craving—expressions of someone wanting me, of someone desiring me. It was intoxicating.

I was immediately in love with this woman and assumed we would be together forever. A month later she moved to Florida and I was left with a broken and tender heart. This was to form the pattern of my relationships—sex leading to a euphoric feeling of love, which lasted only a week or a month ... or even a couple of years.

I completely jumped off the cliff. My train was derailed. If there was a shark, I'd jumped it. And to be clear, I was pretty much happy about it, except for the nagging conscience thing which I would soon beat into submission.

IF LOOKS COULD KILL

Just after I made the final leap off the cliff, Donna came back from Texas and asked me to have lunch with her.

All was going well until she asked me, "So what's this I hear about your new lifestyle choice?"

I don't actually remember this part, but she says my eyes changed and I stared at her with hate. She told her husband, David, if looks could kill, she'd be dead. The eyes looking back at her were not mine, they were being used by the enemy.

She said to me, "Michelle, you know where this road will take you and I will not stop praying for you because you are my friend."

While many moments, situations, and choices in my journey cause me emotional pain, this one ranks near the top. I adored Donna and it is almost unfathomable I would have looked at her with anything other than love. She was my sister, my friend, my mentor, but I threw the relationship away like garbage in my pursuit of fleshly desires.

DESCENT

I became horrified of returning to my home church. I was absolutely terrified. Whenever the thought would come into my head of going back to church, I would immediately think, "Pastor Jim will lay hands on you and this will all end."

By this point in my descent, I was tied fast to the rocket and I was enjoying it all too much to want it to end. The sight of the cross sickened me. I wasn't going to bear my cross, lift a yoke, or engage in any sacrifice. I had only one rule—adult and consensual. This was to be my only guiding principle for the next 20 or so years.

ENDNOTES

1. The research is now clear that viewing and reading pornography literally re-wires the brain and what it finds arousing. http://www.fightthenewdrug.org/porn-affects-your-behavior/
2. Genesis 3:1, NKJV, author's paraphrase.
3. Romans 6:23, NKJV.

CHAPTER 3

Prodigal Running

Sin will take you farther than you want to go, keep you longer than you want to stay, and cost you more than you want to pay.

UNKNOWN

Thus began the years in my life I really don't like to think much about. In the biblical story of the prodigal son the young man demanded his inheritance and ran off to the city. He lived an undisciplined and dissipated life[1]. This is a pretty accurate, if bland, description of the life I lived in my 20s and early 30s.

I was running away from God as fast as my legs would carry me. Nothing can separate us from the love of God[2]—except our own free will. I could run away from God, just as the prodigal son did. God continued to love me, even in my rebellious state, but I was separated from His embrace by my own choice. Because I had spent so much time immersed in the Bible, as well as hearing strong preaching and teaching, I had a finely honed conscience. My conscience was now causing me an immense amount of pain. In order to continue pursuing my hedonistic lifestyle, I had to beat my conscience into silence.

I am not someone who does things halfway or halfheartedly. I throw myself into things with gusto. My pursuit of a life filled with pleasure and experiences was no different.

I craved God, but was terrified of returning to my church and friends. I was afraid of my parents. I was in fear and didn't like it. I became angry. I got into fights and didn't care. I welcomed the release a fight could bring.

During the summer of 1986, I discovered I could do one of three things to make the uncomfortable feelings go away—drink alcohol, fight, or have sex. If I was drinking, I didn't feel anything. If I was fighting or having sex, I only cared about feeling what was happening in the moment. I loved swimming in the feelings released during a fight or sex. To be honest, there weren't many fights. I was keenly aware I could be arrested for fighting and I was truly scared of the prospect.

When I wasn't working, I tried to make sure I was doing one of the other two things. This continued through my first year of college at Emporia State. I had started at ESU thinking I wanted to be a teacher, but still holding on to a dream I'd had for several years of being a doctor. Partway through this first year, I decided I wanted to pursue medical school.

I transferred to the University of Kansas, but spent the summer of 1987 in Kansas City, having the first of many affairs with married women. I enjoyed the power of seducing straight women, releasing in them the desires for woman-to-woman encounters. I believed almost all women were capable of being seduced and would, in fact, enjoy lesbian sex if they'd just let go of their heterosexual and cultural inhibitions.

When I moved to Lawrence, there was a gay bar five minutes from my house. I spent much of my free time there. Not only could I meet women and have sex, I could play pool, and drink beer. Thursdays they played endless gay male porn movies, which I could surreptitiously watch. Studying went by the wayside; there was always tomorrow.

It was at this bar I met several women who invited me into their circle. It was widely believed by these women my arrival in town had been foretold by a psychic they had all visited a month or so earlier. This was certainly appealing to me; the idea I was important enough for a psychic to know about. These women were involved in a mish-mash of New Age spirituality—crystals, psychics, astral projection, spirit travelling, contacting spirits, and spirit guides.

At first, it gave me a sick feeling to be around this type of activity, but I liked belonging in their company so much that I just kept pushing through the feeling. I started carrying a quartz crystal in my pocket and wearing one around my neck. I thought the crystal in my pocket would speak to me, protect me, and warn me. I was still seeking God, but only in the places I wanted to find Him.

THE SPIRIT GUIDE

"Come on, Mick, travel with me," Karrie[3] said to me from the back seat of the car. It was a hot October afternoon and there were four of us in the car.

"How do I do it?" I said.

"Just close your eyes and ask your spirit guide to bring you to me," Karrie answered.

I nodded and closed my eyes. I whispered, "Spirit guide, take me to my friend." Almost immediately my mind was filled with images of an Indian camp and I saw Karrie standing with an Indian chief.

"Wow!" Karrie exclaimed from the back seat, but I barely heard her. I was watching and participating in the scene around me—arrows were flying, people were running, horses galloping.

Karrie reached forward and grabbed my arm, "Mick, come back! Mick, you'll get killed if you stay there!"

I was groggy and reluctant, but I struggled to open my eyes.

"Come back here to me," Karrie commanded. "Come on!"

Finally, I blinked my eyes and sat up straighter. "Ok, I'm back. I'm back. What happened?"

"We were in that camp and they were attacked! I left, but you stayed. I think if you'd been hit with an arrow you would've died there!"

I looked at the clock in the dashboard. Ten minutes had passed.

ALCOHOL AND FOOD

My first semester at KU was an absolute disaster. I failed all my classes because I dropped out without officially withdrawing. I was getting F's in all my classes anyway. Medical school became a failed dream.

It was at this point I also saw the wisdom of joining AA. My girlfriend at the time, Angela, was a recovering alcoholic and she rightly pointed out I had a drinking problem. I also had an eating disorder. When I quit drinking, my food issue became an even more untamable beast.

I had developed certain habits surrounding food when I was in high school. Eating too much and throwing up was the primary one. When I stopped drinking, I was binging and purging on a daily basis. In late November, I was exhausted, out of control, wearied, and scared. I'd quit drinking 30 days prior, but was unable to stop purging.

My parents took me to a hospital in Tulsa, OK, and checked me in to the inpatient eating disorder treatment center. I left 30 days later, no longer binging and purging. I returned to Angela, completely unaware she was having an affair with a co-worker. We lived together for almost two years and I thought it would last forever.

BACK TO COLLEGE

I spent the next few years working at low-end jobs, trying to make ends meet. I hated all of those jobs. I knew the way out of the rut I was in was to go back to school. It took some time, but eventually I re-enrolled at KU and graduated with a degree in English.

I was active on campus with the gay and lesbian political and social groups even before going back to school. I marched for gay rights, protested heterosexual privilege, and engaged in public displays of affection in order to shock mainstream heterosexual people in to acceptance. I pushed to reclaim the word "dyke" and was proud of my identity as a lesbian. When I was mistaken for a boy, I thought it was funny and awesome.

LOVE OF MY LIFE?

I met a woman also named Michelle. She and I were both speakers on a panel, which educated college classes, groups, fraternities, and sororities about homosexuality and discrimination. She was female bisexual representative; I was the lesbian. There were two men on the panel, as well.

Eventually Michelle and I started dating and moved in together. Nine months after we started dating, I decided to ask her to marry me. Marriage wasn't legal for two women, but many homosexual couples had commitment ceremonies and called it a wedding. I scattered rose petals on the floor and taped notes at various locations throughout the huge Victorian we rented. By following the notes, she was able to eventually find me, on one knee, with a ring.

She said no.

I was devastated, hurt, and heartbroken. She still held onto a desire for a heterosexual marriage and children. I felt mortally wounded. In my pride, I knew I should move out immediately, but my fear of being alone was stronger. I stayed with her for another year.

I WAS DEVESTATED, HURT, AND HEARTBROKEN.

ABANDONED MY FAMILY

I abandoned my family. I hardly ever called and visited even less often. My dad had several heart surgeries and I didn't go to the hospital one time. I treated my parents worse than strangers because I was angry and afraid. I didn't want to hear what they had to say about my identity or my choices. It wasn't any of their business so I just avoided them.

I believed I was born gay and deserved to be happy. The Judeo-Christian God and my parents were just being cruel when they tried to prevent me from seeking happiness. Of course, looking back, I see I wasn't happy even if I had moments of happiness.

PORN AGAIN

In my early 20s, (this was before the internet when acquiring porn required some effort) I discovered the "back room" at some video rental stores. These were rooms, which were behind a closed door or more frequently through hanging beads. I would walk confidently into the video store, wander around looking at the mainstream movies, all the while keeping my eye on the back room.

I was looking to see who was in the room, who was in the store, and if anyone was paying particular attention to me or the room. Finally arriving at a level of comfort, heart in my throat, I would slip in and breathe a sigh of relief. Entry and exit were the problematic points—anyone could see me and it was a point beyond my control. Once inside, all was fine. Anyone else in there was like me.

The internet, of course, provided even more relief. I no longer had to go somewhere and take risks to meet my pornography needs. I could merely log on and zone out. I found I could not only watch my ideal partners, but I could write my own porn/erotica. Then I discovered I could sell my stories for money. Writing porn became a secondary addiction. I wanted to meet my favorite porn stars and wanted to be in a porn movie. I even corresponded by email with a couple of these women. It was not odd or awkward. It seemed perfectly natural. The only thing keeping me from pursuing acting in a porn movie was the idea of having sex with a man.

OFF THE CLIFF

Once I was at the point where being in a porn movie was completely acceptable, regardless of parameters, I knew I had driven straight off the cliff. However, I was into thrill-seeking and driving off the cliff was perfectly okay with me. It was a secret from most people who had known me for any length of time, but acceptable with me nonetheless. Those people—mainstream, vanilla people—were just inhibited.

I found all kinds of things acceptable then, not just gay, lesbian and bisexual lifestyles, but transgender, transsexual, gender-bending, casual sex, multiple sex partners, BDSM, polyamory, polygamy, and swinging. As long as it involved consenting human adults, I was fine with it.

I had had sexual encounters with nearly 100 different women and two men. (Both times with men were as part of a threesome with another woman.) I wrote and sold gay, lesbian, and bisexual erotica/pornography. I was addicted to internet and DVD porn—watching for hours if I was at home alone.

SEA OF MEANINGLESSNESS

In religion, as in war and everything else, comfort is the one thing you cannot get by looking for it. If you look for truth, you may find comfort in the end: if you look for comfort you will not get either comfort or truth—only soft soap and wishful thinking to begin with and, in the end, despair.

C. S. LEWIS, MERE CHRISTIANITY

I was, however, still adrift in a sea of meaninglessness. I was frantic for purpose, intentionality, and meaning, but it was elusive. No one I knew seemed to have what I was seeking. It was intense. People who barely knew me would ask my friends, "What is she looking for?" I was obviously on a quest, but I might as well have been wandering in a labyrinth for all the progress I was making.

Eventually I ended up in law school, though certainly not because of any great plan on my part. It was almost an accident, though I now believe God had His hand on me even then. I started law school in Kansas, but hated almost every minute of it. I dropped out and moved to Florida where I discovered a degree in English and one year of law school qualified me to deliver newspapers in the middle of the night.

I searched for a law school which would accept me as a transfer student (most law schools won't), and found one in Kentucky. That was fine with me, I'd been having an online relationship with a married woman from Kentucky. I moved in with her and her husband.

This couple eventually got pregnant and I was very much a part of the pregnancy, birth, and life of the child. He was part of my heart. However, I couldn't remain as a part of the marriage any longer. I had a bed and the husband had a bed. The wife decided each night who she would sleep with. There was one night when she was with me and we were having sex. She jumped out of bed at one point and said, "I need dick" and headed in to his bed instead. Pain and torment fell on me, sickened me, and I sunk in to a swamp of jealousy, envy, and fear.

After graduating from law school, I clerked for a Circuit Judge in Kentucky for a year and a half and worked for Legal Aid in Louisville for a year.

Going to the Dark Side

I began to delve into witchcraft. I became deeply involved in this religion, regularly casting spells and contacting spirits through various means of divination. I dated a woman who was also a witch and had been for over 20 years. Our entire relationship revolved around the lunar cycle, magick (practitioners of witchcraft use the 'k' to identify themselves as real believers rather than pretend), and spells.

At a psychic fair, I met a Native American shaman, and I became apprenticed to her. Shamanism "is a practice that involves a practitioner reaching altered states of consciousness in order to perceive and interact with a spirit world and channel these transcendental energies into this world[4]."I travelled in these altered states of consciousness at least weekly and sometimes daily. I had guides from the other side who fed me information about other people and situations.

ENDNOTES

1. Luke 15:11-32.
2. Romans 8:38
3. Not her real name.
4. Wikipedia contributors. "Shamanism." *Wikipedia, The Free Encyclopedia*. Wikipedia, The Free Encyclopedia, 14 Dec. 2015. Web. 14 Dec. 2015.

CHAPTER 4

Reconnection

I was in law school, living with the married couple, when the phone rang.

"Hello?" I answered.

"Michelle? Michelle Smith?"

"Yes." I recognized the voice and my heart dropped into my stomach.

"This is Pastor Mike Angell, from Emporia."

I hadn't spoken to anyone in my family five years at this point. I figured he was calling to tell me my dad had died.

"How did you find me?"

He laughed, and said, "Well, it wasn't easy, but I did it for your brother. You know, your folks and your brother, they'd really like to talk to you again. Your dad's not doing too well."

It was a shocking conversation, but I agreed to call my folks when I got off the phone with him and I did. I was fearful and the conversations were tentative and sporadic. It took me a couple of years before I could work up the courage to go back home for a visit. I wouldn't go alone and took my girlfriend, Ann, and her daughter, with me. My mom was very warm and welcoming, even loving towards all three of us. I thought perhaps things had changed.

She pulled me aside and said, "Michelle, I love you, and you are all welcome to stay here tonight, but you'll have to sleep in separate rooms."

I was mad, but I understood and appreciated the forewarning. We went to a hotel.

Mom continued to love on us by sending cards and money on birthdays and holidays. I joked it wasn't fair Ann got the same amount of money on her birthday as I did from my parents.

Eventually I returned to Kansas for a position as an assistant prosecutor in Wichita. It was painful leaving the boy who was still part of my heart, as well as Ann and her daughter. I was certain Ann would join me in Kansas after a few months. That never happened and I lost touch with her within the first year of moving.

I became immersed in the black and white law enforcement atmosphere and my search began for normalcy. I was exhausted from my years of frenzied questing for fulfillment. I thought perhaps if I looked in the same places everyone around me looked, then I could find it. Whatever "it" was.

I was beginning to calm down, to live a more stable life, one which wouldn't cause the neighbors to blush. Normal. I thought perhaps

I should also pursue a more normal religious identity. I was still seeking God. I knew I couldn't return to mainstream Christianity, just the thought of it still gave me the heebie-jeebies, but I had a deep longing I couldn't satisfy. I was still writing, reading, and viewing porn. Shortly after moving to Kansas, I entered a relationship with another female attorney, which would last for eight years. It was my longest relationship.

CHAPTER 5

Tentative Steps

It was becoming clearer and clearer if I wanted to come to the end of my life and not say, "I've wasted it!" then I would need to press all the way in, and all the way up, to the ultimate purpose of God and join Him in it. If my life was to have a single, all-satisfying, unifying passion, it would have to be God's passion.

JOHN PIPER

I began studying Kabbalah and the Zohar (both Jewish mysticism) and I decided I needed to talk to a rabbi, to learn as much about the foundational aspects of Judaism as possible before I could truly attain proficiency in Jewish mysticism. At the time, this seemed to fall within the realm of "normal" for me. I met with a rabbi in the Reformed tradition, one who assured me it was okay to continue my life as a practicing lesbian. (I hardly needed the practice. I was quite proficient). Reformed Judaism, he informed me, was open-minded about such things. I began to study Judaism with him, eager to proceed along this path of conversion.

As with everything in my life, I began to read voraciously in this new area of study. This reading led me, rather obviously, to the Bible. Although the thought of entering a Christian church or speaking to any of my former mentors and friends who were Christians almost sickened me, I could read the Bible if I was doing it to pursue Jewish knowledge. I stuck to the Old Testament, which kept me safe from the pesky and disturbing writings of Paul. I couldn't deal with Jesus either, but that was okay for now. He seemed safely ensconced in the New Testament.

What I didn't intend during my course of study was to have feelings about God emerge. I began to sense an awareness of Him again. My previous experiences into other forms of spirituality (or non-spirituality) had always been to soothe an ache, but had always been unsuccessful. They were fun, scary, encouraging, or wishful, but never fulfilling. I began to pray the serenity prayer and the 23rd Psalm. These seemed safe and they were without emotional baggage.

More than a year passed as I met with the rabbi once a week, alone and in a small group. I rarely went to synagogue. I am an introvert by nature, and couldn't seem to break into this Jewish family in any meaningful way. Finally, Rabbi M. told me it was time to pick a date for my official conversion ceremony. He said I was ready.

YOU CAN'T GIVE UP JESUS

Within days of the announcement, I received devastating news. Aunt Jan, dearly beloved and only 11 years older than me, had died unexpectedly. My entire family felt this loss deeply. I drove with my girlfriend to Oklahoma to the funeral.

As I sat in the funeral home chapel, listening to a sermon by a very inexperienced friend of my uncle's, I heard a voice say to me, "You can't give up Jesus."

I turned my head to the left and to the right, but no one was looking at me.

"You can't give up Jesus."

Again, I looked around and no one was paying any attention to me. It repeated again, and perhaps one more time.

I found myself saying, "I can't give up Jesus. I can't give up Jesus."

I FOUND MYSELF SAYING, "I CANT GIVE UP JESUS. I CANT GIVE UP JESUS."

The voice of the minister had faded. I wasn't aware of anything except that thought. I knew to convert to Judaism was to deny Jesus. It turned out I wasn't prepared to to that.

Strangely, even in spite of hearing an audible voice inside my head, I continued to be lost. I searched on the internet for an acceptable church. When I would find a local church which accepted and endorsed the gay lifestyle, I would get excited and go try it out. However, I never went back to any of those churches. It was as if there was a heavy cloud over every single one of them. It was like a giant room lit with only a few 25-watt bulbs. Any church which would accept me as a practicing lesbian lacked all credibility with me. I knew it was wrong, and having someone tell me it was right made me lose all respect for their authority.

Because of my interests and reading in Buddhism, I had discovered Thomas Merton, a Catholic monk who died in 1968. Merton's writings spoke to me:

> In the last analysis, the individual person is responsible for living his own life and for 'finding himself.' If he persists in shifting his responsibility to somebody else, he fails to find out the meaning of his own existence.[1]

This kind of thinking had great appeal to someone like me who was constantly trying to "find myself."

I also began reading theologians in what is called Progressive Christianity such as Marcus Borg and John Shelby Spong. While their theology was appealing to someone who wanted Jesus without sacrifice, Christ without obedience, I was still hungry. The intellectual spin was interesting, but didn't sound the bell of truth in my spirit. I had experienced a relationship with God when I was a child. I longed to be deeply loved and cherished by Him.

ENDNOTE

1. "Thomas Merton." BrainyQuote.com. Xplore Inc, 2015. 14 December 2015. http://www.brainyquote.com/quotes/quotes/t/thomasmert158707.html.

CHAPTER 6

Road to Damascus

"I know the power obedience has of making things easy which seem impossible."

SAINT TERESA OF AVILA

In January 2010 a friend saw me reading a book entitled *Living Buddha Living Christ* by Thich Nhat Hanh. She asked me if I'd ever gone to a Catholic church. I answered no, but I was intrigued by Catholicism.

"Well, you've tried about everything else, why not?"

"Why not, indeed?" I thought. It took me a few months, but eventually I heard about a priest who had a reputation for being very gentle. I called and made an appointment to go meet with Father Jim. This was to be my road to Damascus and I didn't have a clue.

I began meeting with Father Jim in the late summer of 2010. During the first meeting we got acquainted and talked generally about the Catholic Church and how one becomes Catholic. At our second meeting, a week later, I sat in his office petting Toby, the cat. I was focused on the cat rather the priest. Sensing I was nervous or uncomfortable, Father Jim told me the story of Toby, a rescued stray who seemed to have adopted the priest more than the other way around.

"So, Michelle, have you thought any more about becoming Catholic?"

"Yes. Yes, I have, but there's this thing." I took a deep breath, stared at Toby, and said, "I'm a lesbian. I'm gay. So ..." I trailed off.

He didn't lean forward or lean back. He didn't speak too quickly or pause too long. He just nodded and said, "I see. Well, that won't make the church reject you, you can still convert. It's something you will have to confess, but we can discuss it. You can still be Catholic if you want."

His gentle answer brought tears to my eyes.

I went home and struggled. I wanted to be friends with Jesus again. I knew my active homosexuality was a barrier to friendship with Him. I didn't want to ask Jesus to live in me again if I couldn't give myself wholly, but I didn't want to give myself up myself. I understood I did not have to be perfect to come to God; I knew He would accept me and He loved me just as I was. However, because of my journey to this point, I knew that to say yes to Him now meant total obedience. Obedience would only be possible through His grace, but I wanted to be able to say a wholehearted yes this time and not figuratively keep my fingers crossed to create a loophole later.

I was living with my partner. We were purchasing land together, but more important to my consideration was my identity. How could I give up my identity, my essence, my being-ness?

My identity as a lesbian was who I was more than anything else. It defined me, shaped me, and outlined my choices. My friends, my sex, my fantasies, my loves and hates were all intricately interwoven with my lesbian identity. Take the lesbian away and nothing was left but a shell. I had thought of myself as a lesbian first and foremost for so long, I didn't know who I would be if that wasn't my identity.

TAKE THE LESBIAN AWAY AND NOTHING WAS LEFT BUT A SHELL.

It wasn't until later in my journey I discovered God did not condemn the same sex attraction per se. I was not condemned because I experienced sexual/erotic attractions to other women. God condemns the activity of homosexuality. However, my identity is in Christ, not in my attractions—sinful or otherwise.

I also had to come up against all of the theory I had crafted and adopted over the years. I had convinced the Bible didn't mean what it said about homosexuality due to poor translations or cultural differences. When I turned a sharp eye towards this theory, however, I found it fell under a stronger belief. I believed God was good and I believed God said certain things such as, "Be holy as I am holy."[1] I understood the life I'd been living was not holy (consecrated, set aside).

This was a resounding verse for me. This commandment didn't require me to be perfect before I could approach God, but is instead

God's call to me to be consecrated, set apart to Him rather than to my own selfish desires and pursuits. I don't have to be clean to come to God. He will take me just the way I am, but He asks me to give myself to Him. I understood giving myself to Him included being obedient to His instructions. This made sense to me. When I was in a relationship with someone, I knew I was expected to obey the commitment we'd made, whatever it was—no sex outside the relationship, or only sex with someone else if both partners were present, etc.

"It's like being left-handed and being told it's wrong, a sin, to not be right-handed," I complained to my partner, Ariel[2]. As the words left my mouth, a Bible verse popped in to my head: "It's better to enter heaven with one hand than hell with two." As it turned out, it was a paraphrased memory, but incredibly accurate as to the meaning of the original:

> And if your right hand causes you to sin, cut it off and throw it away. For it is better that you lose one of your members than that your whole body go into hell[3].

I also remembered Jesus told someone following Him meant to take up your cross daily[4]. At the time, I understood this to mean carrying your burden daily as a sacrifice. It was clear to me my sexual identity and attractions were my cross.

I thought through the issue logically:

- If I was right and lesbian sex was not a sin, and I continued to have sex with women, I could still go to heaven.

- If I was wrong, and lesbian sex was a sin, and I continued to have sex, I would go to hell. That would equate to another 30-50 years of sex followed by an eternity in hell.
- If I was right and lesbian sex was not a sin, but I did not continue to have sex, I would still go to heaven. That equated to 30-50 years of no sex, but an eternity in heaven.

There are Christians who would say if lesbian sex was a sin and I continued in that lifestyle, I probably wasn't saved in the first place. This is not my personal belief. The Bible is clear that nothing can separate me from God's love[5], however, the Bible is equally clear that God will not violate my free will. I can separate myself from God and He will not force me in to a relationship with Him. He also will not force me to go to Heaven, to dwell in constant relationship with Him if I freely choose to separate myself.

After looking at those statements, the only logical conclusion was to err on the side of caution. I had never stopped believing Jesus died on a cross, was buried, and was resurrected. I never doubted He was coming back. I knew there was a heaven, a hell, and an eternal soul. I tried to forget those things, tried to ignore them, justify them, and get around what they meant and implied, but I didn't deny them. Now, I was being pulled to stare at the bloody cross and decide if I was going to fully and completely embrace it.

I realized I couldn't make God into what I wanted. I had to allow God to make me in to what He wanted.

I COULDNT MAKE GOD INTO WHAT I WANTED.

My struggle at the end of my prodigal days was short-lived. I already knew the answer, had known it for every year of my life, every minute of my existence. I had rationalized, denied, and intellectualized, but I had always known God did not allow women to have sex with other women. I didn't think it was fair. I didn't agree with it, but I knew it was God's rule. When I was 18, I knew to have a relationship with God meant being obedient. I decided then I didn't want the relationship because I didn't want to be obedient.

Now I knew I wanted God. I needed God. Jesus had been pursuing me—sometimes gently, sometimes more persuasively—through the years. I was finally willing to be caught. I went from lesbian to ex-lesbian in less than two weeks. I could not have done this on my own, would have had no reason to.

There is no compelling secular reason not to be a lesbian. Many believers do not understand homosexuality is not like an addiction. I can talk to someone who is addicted to meth and point out her teeth have fallen out, she's lost her kids to the state, and she's homeless. Those are the physical and emotional costs visible to anyone regardless of belief system and without reference to the Bible.

Homosexuality is not like adultery either. One does not need to be a believer in Jesus Christ to count the cost of an affair. I left the lifestyle for Jesus, out of obedience, out of love for the Man on the Throne. This is the only reason someone is going to leave the lifestyle.

Why Does God Say It's Wrong?

Why does God say homosexuality is wrong if there's no compelling secular reason to say it's wrong? Because it's against His ordered creation. He created man and woman for complementarity. Although this quote is referring to the Catechism of the Catholic Church, it is a succinct explanation of complementarity:

> We believe in a God who is a Trinity of Persons, marked by the ecstatic and total self-gift of love between the three divine Persons, as the Catechism explains: "The Holy Spirit proceeds from the Father as the first principle and, by the eternal gift of this to the Son, from the communion of both the Father and the Son" (CCC, 264). This, in turn, is the model for complementary human love in marriage, which contrasts the dualistic framework of the modern "battle of the sexes." [6]

When we choose to go against the natural order as He established it, we are acting contrary to our design. An eye can't be used to hear, no matter how much a person believes it to be so.

AN EYE CAN'T BE USED TO HEAR, NO MATTER HOW MUCH A PERSON BELIEVES IT TO BE SO.

Same sex relationships are a form of idol worship—the worship of one's self as reflected in another. The Lord says, "You have also taken your beautiful jewelry from My gold and My silver, which I had given you, and made for yourself male images and played the harlot with them."[7] We are created in God's image and He is deserving of all worship, adoration, and praise because of who He is—Creator of the universe who sent His son to die in our place, completely sovereign over life, death, and eternity. He loves each of us individually beyond our comprehension. But when we prefer to adore something to the exclusion of Him, or in spite of Him, we are placing something higher than God in our lives. This is idolatry. We can put anything ahead of God—spouse, children, money, possessions, or addictions. With homosexuality, however, we are choosing to worship what we see of ourselves presented in another.

The conversation with Ariel was anticlimactic. God had been dealing with her as well and we agreed to be friends, and only friends, pursuing God. We continued to share a residence, but not a bed, for several months without difficulty.

PEACE COMES THROUGH SURRENDER

> God wants to purify our minds until we can bear all things, believe all things, hope all things and endure all things. God dwells in you, but you cannot have this divine power until you live and walk in the Holy Ghost, until the power of the new life is greater than the old life.
>
> SMITH WIGGLESWORTH

Once I made the decision in my head and heart to agree with God, an intense peace washed over me. God had been pursuing and wooing me my entire life, but at this point, He took hold of me and pulled me to Him. He met me on the road back home, just like the father of the prodigal son. "Draw near to God, and he will draw near to you."[8]

I took one tentative, trembling step towards God and He ran to me. Jesus Himself told the parable of the prodigal son and He said this: "But when he [the lost son] was still a great way off, his father saw him and had compassion, and ran and fell on his neck and kissed him."[9] This is what it looked like when God drew near to me.

What I discovered over the ensuing months was just how many people had been praying for me to return to God. Donna and my mom, of course, but so many others. My mom still attends the same church we did when I was a teenager. When I went back there for the first couple of times, I had many encounters with my mom's prayer warrior friends.

"Hi, you must be new here?"

"Yes, hi. My name's Michelle." Then I would remember I was in Mom's home church and I would add, "Marletta's daughter."

Their eyes would light up, sometimes they would start to cry, and I would usually end up in a huge hug. "Oh! I've been praying for you for so many years!"

Never underestimate the power of prayer, even if the desired result is a long time coming.

TAKING THOUGHTS CAPTIVE

My feelings are not God. God is God. My feelings do not define truth. God's word defines truth. My feelings are echoes and responses to what my mind perceives. And sometimes—many times—my feelings are out of sync with the truth. When that happens—and it happens every day in some measure—I try not to bend the truth to justify my imperfect feelings, but rather, I plead with God:

> Purify my perceptions of your truth
> and transform my feelings so that
> they are in sync with the truth.
>
> JOHN PIPER

Although my intentions to serve God and be obedient were clear, my mind was less than cooperative. Many times, as I sat in church, or when I closed my eyes at night, or when I got bored, images from the past would flood my mind and senses. The imagery and even the physicality was startling in its vividness, clarity, and realism. Unbidden, I would suddenly be watching a memory in my head and it didn't want to turn off. Sometimes it wasn't a memory, but a new fantasy about the person in front of me, without my conscious evocation.

I quickly learned to say, "Get behind me, Satan,"[10] when this happened and to turn my mind's eye to Jesus. I'm not using hyperbole. I literally whispered, "Get behind me, Satan." It was not easy. My brain grooves were comfortable and well-worn, I was used to losing myself in those fantasies, so I was forging new roads in new territory. I saw God's clear instruction: "Submit to God. Resist the devil and he will flee from you."[11] I noted this advice comes clearly ordered—submit, resist, then Satan will flee.

> SUBMIT,
> RESIST,
> THEN SATAN
> WILL FLEE

As I read about the saints of the faith, I discovered this type of spiritual attack wasn't unique to me.

St. Josemaria Escriva said, "To defend his purity, St. Francis of Assisi rolled in the snow, St. Benedict threw himself into a thorn bush, St. Bernard plunged into an icy pond ... You ... what have you done?"[12]

> In temptations against chastity, the spiritual masters advise us, not so much to contend with the bad thought, as to turn the mind to some spiritual, or, at least, indifferent object. It is useful to combat other bad thoughts face to face, but not thoughts of impurity.[13]
>
> ST. ALPHONSUS LIGUORI

When I found this quote from Liguori I experienced a turning point—I learned to not fight the tempting thought because that just puts my focus all the more on it. Instead, I started turning my thoughts to something else entirely. This is a skill, just like serving a volleyball or balancing a drink tray, and it takes practice. In the beginning all I could do was literally move my eyes to some inanimate object and start mentally describing it. "The vase is slender, blue, glass. The flower is yellow." As I continued to practice, I could eventually call forth scripture or envision the cross. I learned not to linger, not to try to get a little enjoyment out of the image or thought before turning my attention, but to do so immediately.

TOOLS TO BOLSTER RESOLVE

"Not having my own righteousness, which is from the law, but that which is through faith in Christ, the righteousness which is from God by faith."[14] I am not made righteous through works. The discussion that follows does not imply otherwise.

I discovered quickly many television shows and movies contain lesbian scenes of kissing and/or sexual activity. Because those scenes immediately cause a physical and emotional response, I chose early in my walk with Jesus to avoid them. I do not choose to watch television or movies without someone I trust telling me it's safe for me to do so. I consider my viewing and entertainment practices through one lens—does it enhance your relationship with Christ or detract from it? Do the thoughts and images intrude into your quiet time with the Lord?

Another tool I learned to use early in my return was confession. Obviously, this is an aspect of Catholicism of which everyone is aware. However, I learned it is Scriptural and necessary to every believer. When I was Catholic, I made use of the confessional on a regular and consistent basis, making confession of large and small sins, learning through the priest's guidance what was a sin and what wasn't (for instance, dreams of sexual activities aren't a sin but lingering on them in the waking hours is).

Once I was no longer Catholic, I knew I still needed the accountability. I chose Donna, my oldest friend and trusted mentor, to be my sounding board. Not like I used the priest, not for absolution, but because we are told to "confess your sins to each other and pray for each other so that you may be healed."[15]

For example, about three years after I'd come back to God, I was watching a British television series on Netflix. It had not been previewed by anyone I knew and I could tell there was a building story line between two of the female characters, which might lead to something sexual. I continued watching episodes until there was indeed a very sensual scene between the two women.

I didn't stop there though. I hit rewind and watched the scene two more times. Then I found myself on the internet watching similar scenes from television shows. I did stop, but I lost myself for 15-30 minutes. I felt sad and guilty, but when I got up the next morning, the first thing I did was text Donna and confess. Her words of support and kindness brought me out of my self-imposed guilt, reminding me that God's forgiveness is immediate when we ask for it. He doesn't withhold it while we feel bad just to teach us a lesson. We aren't sent to our room or grounded. Ask forgiveness, commit to changing the behavior, and move forward.

GOD DOESN'T WITHHOLD FORGIVENESS WHEN WE FEEL BAD JUST TO TEACH US A LESSON.

I could not utilize any of these tools, however, without God's grace. Grace is God's gift to His children which empowers, strengthens, and enables each believer to live like Christ. Without grace, we are incapable of choosing the good[16].

> We have peace with God through our Lord Jesus Christ, through whom also ***we have access by faith into this grace*** in which we stand.[17]

> Faith is the determining factor for whether we do or do not partake of grace. This means grace cannot be accessed any other way than through faith. Now, let me reiterate this fact: Grace is the empowerment needed to please God. Therefore we are told: "Without faith it is impossible to please God."[5]

AND WE DANCED

I completed my conversion to Catholicism at Easter at the Saturday night Mass. It is a long, solemn proceeding culminating with converts taking Communion for the first time. This was the completion of nine months of study and prayer for me. When I first agreed with God's rules about my sexuality, I could not physically bend my knee to Him. It's like I was saying I would obey, but I would not serve, would not humble myself before Him. The Catholic Church, with her kneelers and prescribed times during service to take a knee, helped me past this block. By the time I got to the first Easter, I was fully prepared to kneel on stones in order to express my acceptance of His Lordship over my life.

I knelt in prayer, waiting for my turn to approach Father Jim and take communion. When I finally took the Host into my mouth, I felt overwhelmed and tears filled my eyes. I returned to my seat and fell to my knees, thanking Jesus for His love and His sacrifice. My head filled with a vision. I was dressed in a flowing white dress in the middle of a field. Jesus came towards me with His hand outstretched. I took His hand and He pulled me into an embrace and then a dance. I danced with Jesus and wanted it to last forever!

God Heals the Broken

During my first year of being back with God, one of my frequent prayers was, "Dear Jesus, I know I'm broken, but please use me anyway." I was thoroughly saddened and repentant for my many errors—not just the misuse of my sexuality, but pride, arrogance, lost time, and more.

One time when I was praying that prayer I saw a vision of a small ceramic pot hanging on a stick over a campfire. It fell into the fire and cracked all down one side. It was filled with cold ashes from the fire. I started crying because I knew it was me. Then a hand appeared and gently picked the pot up and turned it so I could see inside. The crack ran all the way from top to bottom and was visible inside, as well as out. The inside was filthy with ashes.

As I was wondering how it could ever be useful again, a finger ran gently, but firmly down the crack, sealing it. Then a deep breath blew into the pot, completely cleansing it of ashes. I knew it was the breath of God. "I have healed you, you are no longer broken, and My breath will free you from the ashes."

I spent many hours reading old writings from the Christian tradition—Aquinas, Augustine, St. John of the Cross, St. Teresa of Avila, and many others. Two of my favorite books were *The Sinner's Guide* by Venerable Louis of Grenada (published in 1555) and *The School of Jesus Crucified* by Father Ignatius of the Side of Jesus, Passionist, (published in 1895) but Teresa of Avila's writings led me onward in my quest to know more about who Jesus is on a personal level. Kempis' *Imitation of Christ* has also been instructive.

I ached to know—really know—Jesus, in the way one knows one's best friend. I wanted to be a friend of God. I started my journey back to God with trepidation and a refusal to bend my knee. I soon learned the joy of giving myself wholly over to be a "slave of Christ." [19] As I prayed and sought Him from that posture, I found myself growing in to a servant. From servant, I learned to see myself as an adopted child of Father God, then a friend, and finally as part of the Bride of Christ. It is not a linear progression, and I believe I am all of these—slave, servant, child, friend, bride—in my relationship with Him. Each is an identity with an eye firmly focused on Jesus; my identity is in Him and in no other.

Finding my identity in anything other than Him is to fall into idolatry. Idolatry is bestowing on another being or thing the reverence, adoration, and priority due and reserved to God alone.

ENDNOTES

1. 1 Peter 1:16.
2. Not her real name.
3. Matthew 5:30
4. Matthew 16:24
5. Romans 8:38-39.
6. http://www.catholicworldreport.com/Item/4158/the_complementarity_of_men_and_women_across_the_religious_spectrum.aspx
7. Ezekiel 16:17.
8. James 4:8.
9. Luke 15:20.
10. Matthew 16:23
11. James 4:7
12. *The Way*, Saint Josemaria Escriva, #143, Scepter Pubs (January 1, 1992)

13. *Sermons of St. Alphonsus Liguori: For All the Sundays of the Year,* St. Alphonsus Liguori, TAN Books; 4th edition (January 1, 1952).
14. Phillipians 3:9
15. James 5:16.
16. 2 Corinthians 12:9.
17. Romans 5:1-2, emphasis added.
18. John Bevere, "John Bevere: Why Are Christians Forgetting About Grace?", 11/17/13, http://www.charismanews.com/opinion/41736-grace-the-big-disconnect.
19. Romans 6:16.

I AM ALL OF THESE IN MY
RELATIONSHIP WITH HIM:

SLAVE
SERVANT
CHILD
FRIEND
BRIDE

CHAPTER 7

Full Circle

As for myself, I have found my perfect pattern in Jesus, who said, "The Father has not left Me alone, for I always do those things that please Him." I am no longer motivated by personal ambition. I have discovered a sweeter, purer motive: simply to please my Father.

DEREK PRINCE

Soon after I made the decision to start walking towards God by being obedient to His directives, I called my old youth pastors—David and Donna.

"Hello," David answered.

"Uh ... hi ... this is Michelle. Smith. From Kansas?"

"Sure, Michelle, how are you?"

"I'm good. Is Donna there? This is the only number my mom had for you guys."

"She's out of the country, do you need anything or just want me to tell her you called?"

"Well, yeah, I have some good news, you know. I'm back with God." I was halting in my delivery because it was all still new and I really didn't have any words for my experiences.

"Praise Jesus!" His words exploded in my heart. "Donna's been praying for you every day all of these years!"

Tears welled up in my eyes. To think she'd cared enough about me to continue praying for 20 plus years was beyond my comprehension.

In December of 2011 I was able to go to Emporia to spend the evening at Mike and Jannie's home with David and Donna. It's funny how ties and connections can remain strong even through such turbulent waters as I traveled. Jannie's dad was Pastor Kegin, and Mike and I went to high school together. I was present at the youth group meeting when Mike accepted Christ. All the girls had a secret crush on Mike, I think, but it seemed he only had eyes for Jannie from very early on. Mike and Jannie now serve as pastors of the church Pastor Kegin founded.

I was overwhelmed by the love I experienced from all four of them. Swept up and in, welcomed, loved, and accepted. I was not judged or resented for the years I was running. They prayed over me and for me, spoke words of prophesy I don't remember, and it all took me back to those happy, joyous moments 20 odd years ago when we'd all been together in almost the exact same formation. There is something to be said for history!

RETURNING TO THE FAITH OF MY YOUTH

In any event, this experience brought me full circle and I realized I wasn't getting all I wanted from my Catholicism. I craved more. I craved even more intimacy with Jesus and I wanted to share His love with others. I cannot say enough how grateful I am for Father Jim and the other faithful Catholics who opened their hearts and doors to me, giving me a hand as I left one path and stepped onto another.

The foundational reading I did during my time in the Catholic Church served and continues to serve me in my daily life, in my apologetics, and in my evangelism efforts. Teresa of Avila and John of the Cross as well as some other lesser known writers will forever be part of my posse.

I began to seek out a church which was more Pentecostal/Charismatic. Mike recommended three he knew about in Wichita. True to my personality, I chose to try the one Mike identified as "it might be too fiery for you." Because of how this brief period in my life concludes, I will not identify the church or the denomination. The first night there, I liked it, but was uncertain. I seemed to have a strange feeling about the pastor's wife, but I chalked it up to nervousness at being in this type of environment again. It was a very small church, hardly ever more than 30 people in attendance on a Sunday morning, but warm and welcoming.

After three weeks of attending both this church and the Catholic Church, I stopped attending Mass. Ariel and I had many tear-stained conversations as she believed I was certainly making a wrong decision by leaving the Catholic Church.

By the Spring of that year, I was regularly attending Sunday morning, Sunday evening, Wednesday evening and Saturday evening services at the new church. Unfortunately, within a few months, I was falsely accused of having an affair with the pastor. I was horrified.

I WAS HORRIFIED. I FLED.

I fled. I drove to my mom's in Emporia and spent most of the weekend on the couch at Mike and Jannie's house. I told Mike I was placing myself under obedience to him, I would do whatever he told me to do regarding this situation. He advised me to remove myself completely and I did. I stopped attending that church and cut all ties with any of the members except for one friend. I was completely cut adrift.

I clung to my Jesus even more. I remembered something Donna told me in the very first email she sent me after I'd returned to Jesus. "Don't blame God for the behavior of His children."

CHAPTER 8

Forgiveness Through Jesus

Forgiveness is the key that unlocks the door
of resentment and the handcuffs of hatred.
It is a power that breaks the chains of
bitterness and the shackles of selfishness.

CORRIE TEN BOOM

In addition to learning obedience, I also had to practice forgiveness. I had a catalog of wrongs and hurts perpetrated against me. I was a victim. I was a survivor. In spite of … Each of those identities was a charm on the bracelet that imprisoned me. I had gone through traditional therapy, as well as numerous other New Age techniques to get rid of old baggage. I had confessed and counselled and acted "as if." I had written names on paper and burned it at midnight. Still, though, I had triggers, lingering memories, and a definite angry sadness about the past.

One very clear example of my lack of forgiveness was my utter inability to stand next to my mom in church. We had made amends, vowed our love, and offered apologies and forgiveness to one another. I considered her a loving mother but I could not make myself be in church with her.

Five months after seeing David and Donna in Emporia, I traveled to Texas to visit them and their Bible school in Mexico. While I was there, Donna walked me through forgiving others through the great Forgiver.

"Now, Michelle, you know we have to forgive, right?"

"Sure. The Bible is clear about that. I've forgiven everyone."

She smiled. "Well, isn't it more you've tried to forgive and done everything to forgive, but just can't fully get there?"

I acknowledged that was more accurate. I'd done everything I could and gotten as far as I could and figured this was as good as it was going to get.

"Is anything impossible for Jesus?" She asked.

"Of course not."

"So He can forgive anyone for anything, right?"

"Yes."

"When you've tried to forgive before, you've always tried to do it yourself, with your own willpower, right?"

"Yes, I guess so."

"I don't believe that's what we're supposed to do. I believe we need to take each person to Jesus and let Him forgive, handing out justice and grace as He sees fit. He's perfect, right?"

"Right," I said, thinking.

"Where does Jesus live?"

"In me."

"Put your hands over your center, where He lives. Now, close your eyes and see Him."

She then led me through thinking about each of the major players in my catalog of wrongs. My mom was first on my list. I brought the person to mind, relived the experience (or at least a representation of a category of experiences), felt the pain again, then walked the person to Jesus. I gave (shoved) the person to Jesus, asking Him to forgive the person because I couldn't. Finally, I asked Him for forgiveness for my own reactions to the situation or person.

FRUITS OF FORGIVENESS

I returned to Kansas on a Saturday. I called Mom and asked her to come down and go to church with me the next day. I not only attended church with mom, I stood and sat next to her the entire service, without even a twinge of discomfort. Jesus took the burden I'd been carrying for so long.

Forgiving others through the Great Forgiver is now a weekly, if not daily, staple of my walk with God. The moment I realize I'm feeling offended, angry, or hurt at something someone has done, I get alone with God and drop down. I take the person to Jesus and allow Him to do the work I can't in my own human frailty.

I have also led a number of people through this same exercise and each one has experienced great freedom and healing. I was in Mexico City with Donna on an outreach for a week and we did several of these sessions with individuals who approached Donna for deliverance or physical healing. Without exception, after giving up the claim to justice or anger or bitterness, each person received a physical healing in their body.

Unforgiveness is debilitating.

> See to it that no one fails to obtain the grace of God; that no "root of bitterness" springs up and causes trouble, and by it many become defiled[1].

Furthermore, Jesus very clearly tells us we are forgiven in the same way and to the same degree that we forgive others.

> For if you forgive other people when they sin against you, your heavenly Father will also forgive you[2].

ENDNOTES

1. Hebrews 12:15.
2. Matthew 6:14.

CHAPTER 9

The Call

> The truth is that the Spirit of the living God is guaranteed to ask you to go somewhereor do something you wouldn't normally want or choose to do. The Spirit will lead you into the way of the cross, as He led Jesus to the cross, and that is definitely not a safe or pretty or comfortable place to be. The Holy Spirit of God will mold you into the person you were made to be.
>
> FRANCIS CHAN

I went to Kansas City with two of my friends to a Prophetic Evangelism seminar at the International House of Prayer (IHOP) in 2013. On the second day, as we sat near the front waiting for the day's worship and teaching to get started, I saw a man come in who couldn't seem to take his eyes off me. He had not been there the previous day. He just kept staring at me. I smiled, but he was just very intense.

Hal Lindhardt introduced him as Rodney, the first speaker of the day.

As he took the microphone, he said, "God woke me up at 5:30 this morning with the message that there would be someone here who was powerfully called to the homosexual people group." He then looked directly at me.

I put my hand in the air, palm towards him in a warding gesture, and said, "I'm not talking to you." I started crying and I turned to my friend, Jen, and said, "I don't want this." I collapsed in sobs. God was doing a great work in me. Up to this point, my biggest fear was that God would want me to be an evangelist to people in the gay and lesbian lifestyle.

UP TO THIS POINT, MY BIGGEST FEAR WAS THAT GOD WOULD WANT ME TO BE AN EVANGELIST TO PEOPLE IN THE GAY AND LESBIAN LIFESTYLE.

Hal and Rodney asked for the whole room to stretch out their hands and pray for me.

Within moments, I looked up, embarrassed but empowered by God's grace to say yes. They asked me and anyone else called to the LGBT (Lesbian, Gay, Bisexual, Transgendered) people group to come forward for prayer and activation. The Spirit of God landed heavily on me and when I fell under the weight of it, I took all of the other people with me (and a drum set). We all ended up in a pile on the floor.

MINISTRY

Ministry is not about where you are or where you go, it is about where He is.

HEIDI BAKER

I had had several opportunities to minister to others who are in the homosexual lifestyle or are struggling with issues surrounding the Bible's teaching in this area. I have met individually with people, dialogued online, spoken to groups of women eager to understand how to relate to people in this lifestyle, and I have engaged in street outreach at gay pride parades.

It is important to remember that Truth and Love is required in this ministry—God's Truth balanced with God's Love.[1] All Truth and no Love creates an atmosphere of condemnation, judgment, and anger. It is unsuccessful and does not exhibit God's love for all people. All Love and no Truth creates an atmosphere of permissiveness, greasing the slide to hell. The churches who have opted to disregard clear Biblical truth in order to fully embrace the homosexual lifestyle are examples of this.

Truth and Love, however, is biblical. When I have been out on the street or in the bars at gay pride events, speaking to people, they know without me saying it I'm not one of the permissive Christians. Their concern is whether I'm one of the hateful Christians. I quickly assure them I am not.

"We're just out here to apologize for how the church and some Christians have treated gay people. It was mean and wrong. Jesus loves you. The Bible says we have all sinned and fallen short, every one of us, but he loves everyone of us and he wants every person to come to Him, to have eternal life with Him. That's why He came to earth and died on the cross. Because we've all sinned, each of us has to ask for forgiveness. No one is better than someone else."

This approach of Love and Truth has been successful and, in most cases, appreciated.

At one event, I sat at a picnic table with another missionary to this people group, a man who had come out of the gay lifestyle. We were one pair of 50 who were available to dialogue with anyone who wanted to talk to us.

"Hey," I said in greeting to the woman who sat down across from us. She was casually dressed, but had a professional demeanor.

"Hi. I'm Claire. I'm a radical queer woman."

It was quite the introduction, but I just chuckled and stuck out my hand to shake.

Once she realized Zack and I were both laid back and nice, she was able to relax somewhat.

"I'm the director of my church's children's ministry and my church says its fine to be queer."

I nodded and asked God in my mind to guide me. Her partner joined us and she introduced him as Mike. I observed Mike was a female presenting to the world as a male. Mike, with tears in his eyes, told us about working as a camp counselor with kids who were suicidal because of the hatred the church taught.

I proceeded to give the five-minute version of my testimony. I did not argue with them about what the Bible said, I didn't try to argue natural law, and I didn't tell them they were wrong and going to hell. I spoke to them from my heart with love and compassion.

Claire had tears in her eyes and one rolled down her cheek.

"What's going on right now?" I asked.

"I'm just so sad for you," she said.

I laughed and took her hand. "Oh, thank you, that's so sweet, but completely unnecessary! I am so content now. I won't lie to you and tell you I was miserable and depressed when I was in the life, but now I'm walking in so much of Jesus' love for me, I'm okay. Really."

I don't know if she believed me. However, I do know Claire and Mike experienced something they had not previously, namely, Love and Truth. I have every confidence Holy Spirit can and will use such small beginnings to work in their lives, pursuing them. I pray I will get a chance to meet them both in Heaven.

If you are a Christian who wants to minister to someone in this lifestyle, you should have your own house in order. I'm not saying you should be sinless, but you shouldn't be actively involved in compromise. If you are reading "mommy porn" or enjoying salacious movies you have no authority to call out someone else's sin.

I think that the Bible teaches that homosexuality is a sin, but the Bible also teaches that pride is a sin, jealousy is a sin, and hate is a sin, evil thoughts are a sin. So I don't think that homosexuality should be chosen as the overwhelming sin that we are doing today.

BILLY GRAHAM

ENDNOTE

1. I capitalize Truth and Love in this context because I mean God's Truth and Love, not merely what individual human beings understand of those two words. I am referring to the Truth written on our hearts by God and the Love large enough to encompass Jesus' sacrifice.

CHAPTER 10

Identity

Truth is not obtained cheaply. It demands much time given to prayer and study of the Scriptures, followed by practical application in our daily lives. It must take priority over the many forms of cheap entertainment offered by our secular culture. It is a lifetime commitment.

DEREK PRINCE

I say I used to be gay not because I'm now in love with a man, feel particularly heterosexual, never have temptations, or think I've somehow been promised a fulfilling and satisfying marriage to man. I sometimes miss the emotional support I received when I lived with a woman. I don't know if I could be married to a man—living with him and engaging sexually with him. However, I've given it to God, as my confidence in His ability to decide those issues is complete.

I do not identify as a gay Christian. Homosexuality has nothing to do with my identity. My identity is in Christ, as a child of God, an heir to the Kingdom. To call myself a gay Christian is to qualify my identity in Christ, to say something about my sexuality is on the same level as my adoption into God's family. It also leaves open a door to justification. I've heard many gay Christians in the past say any sex outside of marriage is wrong, therefore, they are chaste gay Christians. Now that the law of the land accepts and approves of same sex marriage, does that create a cognitive dissonance for those gay Christians?

HOW TO LIVE LIFE

It's crazy, if you think about it. The God of the universe—the creator of nitrogen and pine needles, galaxies and E-minor—loves us with a radical, unconditional, self-sacrificing love. And what is our typical response? We go to church, sing songs, and try not to cuss.

FRANCIS CHAN

I believe Jesus is the Son of God. He came to earth to live a sinless life and die as a perfect sacrifice for me. He did in fact die and was resurrected 3 days later. He is in heaven and intercedes for me with God the Father. Believing these things, my heart is set on being a disciple and friend of Jesus. The scriptures provide guidance to being a disciple. There is a piece of scripture which is widely referred to as the Great Commission. It was Jesus' prime directive to his disciples after His resurrection. He tells them to go out in to all the world and make disciples1. By this I understood Jesus desires disciples. A disciple is someone given wholeheartedly to something. A disciple is more than a fan, but is someone who is sold out, in this case, to Jesus.

"Whoever does not bear his cross and come after Me cannot be My disciple."[2] I had already accepted that to bear my cross was to sacrifice everything within myself to Him. I was willing to lay my very self as I knew it on the altar and give it to Him to do with as He willed. I did not view myself as my own[3].

I further read "If you abide in My word, you are My disciples indeed."[4] Jesus said, "If you keep my commandments, you shall abide in my love; as I also have kept my Father's commandments, and do abide in his love."[5] These are deep verses with multiple layers but first and foremost, when read together, they speak clearly to me of delving deeply in to the word of God, the Bible, and following His commandments. He speaks promises throughout scripture, promises of eternity, of divine love and forgiveness, and of adoption into the family of God.

Jesus was asked what the greatest commandment was and He answered, "Love the Lord your God with all your heart and with all your soul and with all your mind."[6] How can I express such love and devotion if I am constantly doing what He has asked me not to do? If I am always looking for a loophole in His love, do I love Him with all my mind?

IF I AM ALWAYS LOOKING FOR A LOOPHOLE IN HIS LOVE, DO I LOVE HIM WITH ALL MY MIND?

> And by this we know that we have come to know him, if we keep his commandments. Whoever says "I know him" but does not keep his commandments is a liar, and the truth is not in him, but whoever keeps his word, in him truly the love of God is perfected. By this we may know that we are in him: whoever says he abides in him ought to walk in the same way in which he walked[7].

WHO GOD IS

> You cannot hold God hostage (to your questions). He doesn't owe you an answer. If you want the peace that passes understanding, you're going to have to give up your right to understanding. It's called trust.
>
> BILL JOHNSON

I have been learning—daily—over the last five years that He is my El Shaddai, my All-Sufficient. He is who I turn to when the loneliness sets in, when I feel doubt or fear, when I don't feel loved, or feel too dirty, too far gone, incapable, unusable.

I get up every morning, eager to walk in obedience to God who loves me. I have a relationship with Him, a relationship I pursue every day. I am far from perfect, but because of my friendship with God, because I know who I am in Him and that Christ is in me, I strive towards my calling. We are each called to holiness. Be holy as the Lord your God is holy.

I seek a deepening friendship with God, not heterosexuality. If I keep my focus on my relationship with God, then nothing else matters.

I take every thought captive[8]. I have taken this instruction to heart. I found early in my transformation any lesbian relationship on television or in movies was a temptation. These visuals evoked the old feelings of lust and longing. When thoughts, feelings, or images come into my head, I say no immediately and turn my attention towards Jesus. People will have a problem with what I've just said. They will tell me it's not healthy to squelch desire, but I say it's not healthy to give a crazy horse its head.

There are any number of stories out there of people who walked in the ex-gay movement, but have returned to the homosexual lifestyle, just as there are stories of Christian leaders announcing they are now gay. The problem isn't homosexuality, it's any disobedience to God is sin. It's a refusal to walk in obedience. One doesn't come to the conclusion the Bible doesn't say what it says or it doesn't mean what it plainly says without conscious effort to find a loophole for one's own desires.

The truth is written on my heart[9]. When I become full of pride, I lose my ability to hear truth. I develop an ability to justify what I want as other than plain old sin. I now live without fear that I'm living in disobedience and rejecting God's blessing. I live in the presence of His love.

MY LIFE TODAY

My life today is amazing. I have a deep peace about my place in the world. It hasn't been a quick and automatic transformation. I've had to work for it. With God's help, however, it has never been impossible or even troublesome. He has provided me with friends to love me and support me. He has provided me with a mentor who is off the charts awesome. I have found Godly mentors in the writings of His other children, both living and dead.

I have a job I love representing children and I work with people I like and respect. I am the very proud and blessed foster mom to a beautiful, funny, smart, tough, and tender little two-year-old boy. God willing and the creek don't rise, I'll be adopting him in the next 12 months and the blessing is all mine.

I am not dating and I am not married. I've struggled with this. Truly struggled and agonized with God about why not. I'm interested and open to meeting the man God has for me, but it hasn't happened. Maybe it is a "not yet" or maybe it's a "will not," but in any event what I've learned through this is God is my All-Sufficient in everything, in every aspect and area of my life. I have had to learn to depend on Him. If I had met a man right away and gotten married I would have learned to depend on my husband and not my God.

GOD IS MY ALL-SUFFICIENT IN EVERYTHING.

When I was in my early 20s, I got a tattoo on my shoulder declaring my lesbianism. It was bold and a definite statement to the world. Shortly after coming back to God, I got a cover up tattoo. The new tattoo is the sacred heart of Jesus, burning in His love for me. I am constantly being refined in His fire.

Thank you, Jesus, I am so grateful for my life!

ENDNOTES

1. Matthew 28:19
2. Luke 14:27
3. 2 Corinthians 6:19-20.
4. John 8:31.
5. John 15:7.
6. Matthew 22:37.
7. 1 John 2:3-6.
8. 2 Corinthians 10:5.
9. Jeremiah 31:33; Psalm 119:11; Romans 2:15.

CHAPTER 11

To My Younger Self...

Hey, kid—

You are so torn up inside. You are fighting this secret battle and quite frankly, you are completely unarmed and missing most of your armor. You want to trust someone, you want to feel deeply loved, and you are so afraid. You don't have to be though. You don't have to be tough and ashamed. You think you understand who God is, but you have only the most basic knowledge of Him. You've forgotten what it was like to walk in the countryside, alone except for Jesus, talking to Him and sharing your thoughts, dreams, and fears. You need to learn who God is really—a loving Father who is ever-present and loves you so much it's completely mind-blowing! You can give Him all that shame and fear; He'll take it, I swear.

Don't do something for the experience or to justify your existence.

Don't try something just to see if it feels wrong. Feelings lie and change and mutate all the time. You shouldn't base decisions on how something feels or how you think it might feel.

Seek God. Seriously. Seek Him. Like you would someone you had a crush on. Peek around the corners, find out His schedule, put yourself in His path, think about Him all the time. Ask yourself what would He say? What would He like? What would He say?

When you're seeking Him, talk to Him. Don't just ask Him to take something away and please watch over my loved ones. Is that how you talk to anyone else? Be real, just talk to Him. It'll get easier.

Finally, stop keeping secrets. They will eventually eat you up from the inside. Call Donna, tell her you need to a couple of hours to talk. Tell her what's going on with you. All of it. Everything. Lay it out. She might not have any answers you like or even seem helpful, but it will help.

You won't like where this road is leading you; trust me, I've been down it all the way.

Love,
Me/You

P.S. You are beautiful, smart, and funny. Tell yourself that every time you look in the mirror instead of all the other garbage.

CHAPTER 12

To Christian Leaders

Christians Who Say Homosexuality Is Not a Sin

I'm certain that you believe you are doing the right thing. I've read your words and spoken to a few of you—Christian leaders who have decided that homosexuality is not a sin. You are well-meaning, loving, and sincere. Most often you have a family member who is LGBT, a child, a sibling, or maybe a close friend. You've seen the pain and struggle and you've decided that it is in your power to make it better, to ease the suffering.

This is a decision you have made on a personal level which you have then promulgated publicly. I hope that this book has spoken to you from the other side of the issue. I, and so many others like me, are warring to stand with God. We war against our flesh and we war against the culture at large. Finally, we have to face Christian pastors and leaders who have decided that our battle is meaningless.

By espousing the lie that homosexuality is not a sin, you have betrayed every brother and sister in Christ who lays down their sexuality on the altar of obedience every day.

My brethren, let not many of you become teachers, knowing that we shall receive a stricter judgment.

JAMES 3.1

CHAPTER 13

Come to Jesus

Because of our sin, we are separated from God.

For all have sinned and fall short
of the glory of God.

ROMANS 3.23

The Penalty for our sin is death.

"For the wages of sin is death,
but the gift of God is eternal life
in Jesus Christ our Lord."

ROMANS 6.23

The penalty for our sin was paid by Jesus Christ!

But God demonstrates His own love toward us, in that while we were yet sinners, Christ died for us.

ROMANS 5.8

If we repent of our sin, then confess and trust Jesus Christ as our Lord and Savior, we will be saved from our sins!

For whoever calls on the name of the Lord shall be saved.

ROMANS 10.13

If you confess with your mouth the Lord Jesus and believe in your heart that God has raised Him from the dead, you will be saved. For with the heart one believes unto righteousness, and with the mouth confession is made unto salvation.

ROMANS 10.9-10

Coming to Jesus for the first time or coming back to Him after a season of being a prodigal is as easy as a whispered prayer. Please say this prayer now.

> Dear Jesus, I believe you are the Son of God, you died as payment for my sins, and you were raised from the dead. I want you to live in me, Jesus, to be my friend, and I want to be yours. Forgive me for the things I've done, I know I've sinned. Please send the Holy Spirit to help me to do better.

CONGRATULATIONS! WELCOME TO THE FAMILY.

Now, you will want to find a good, Bible-believing church. Introduce yourself to the pastor and briefly explain you are a new believer or a newly returning one. This would be a good time to ask if there is a discipleship program so you can get connected to more mature believers.

Don't keep your struggles a secret. It's perfectly acceptable to want to keep your past private, but you will wither and die if you try to carry everything alone. Find one or two people in your church that you can confide in. Start with the pastor and let him or her direct you to others.

WORTH A THOUSAND WORDS

Photo Testimony

I wanted to share just a few photos with you. They are telling of my journey into the LGBT lifestyle and the transformation which has occurred since I ran into the arms of Jesus.

Michelle with her adoptive father, Carl Smith

Living an "Active" Lifestyle in the 80s

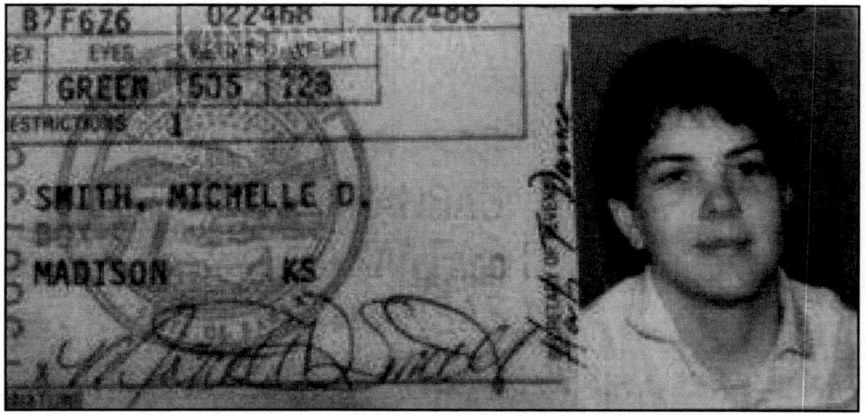

Driver's License Photo 1988

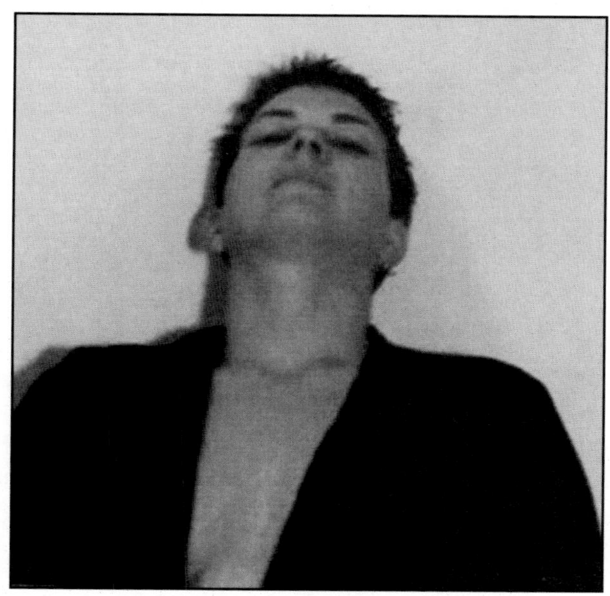

Taken by a Girlfriend (Around 1993)

Officially an Attorney (1999)

Just before my talk with Father Jim

Christmas 2009

Side by side: In the Lifestyle ... Just Out of the Lifestyle

Michelle in 2016, Writing *Prodigal Pursued*

THE LORD GIVES HIS PEOPLE
PERPETUAL JOY WHEN THEY
WALK IN OBEDIENCE TO HIM.

-DWIGHT L. MOODY

JOY IS PRAYER; JOY IS STRENGTH:
JOY IS LOVE; JOY IS A NET OF LOVE
BY WHICH YOU CAN CATCH SOULS.

-MOTHER TERESA

YOU HAVE LET ME EXPERIENCE
THE JOYS OF LIFE AND THE
EXQUISITE PLEASURES OF YOUR
OWN ETERNAL PRESENCE.

-PSALM 16:11 (NLB)

MEET THE AUTHOR

Michelle X. Smith

LEFT THE LIFESTYLE TO LIVE WITH JESUS

Michelle is a practicing attorney and was an Assistant District Attorney for eight years. Prior to that she maintained a solo practitioner law firm as a criminal defense attorney for two years and is currently representing children who are involved in abuse or neglect court cases.

An adopted child, Michelle knows the blessing of being taken in and loved by parents. She is in the process of adopting her two and a half year old foster son, and knows without a doubt that he is a blessing and a gift from Father God!

Michelle has participated in several street evangelism events including LGBT Pride events. She has volunteered with both Trinity Works in Minneapolis and IHOP Kansas City in evangelism events. She understands the importance of pairing evangelism with intercession and worship and is committed to sharing God's love entwined with God's truth.

PRODIGAL PURSUED MINISTRIES

Michelle felt God calling her to launch a deliverance and education ministry called Prodigal Pursued to coordinate her outreach efforts to the sexually broken, specifically the LGBT people group. She is an evangelist who has a heart to reach the lost and hurting.

God's call on her is not just to touch the LGBT community, but also to reach out to the Church, to share a message of hope to Christians who feel they have lost a loved one to the LGBT lifestyle. She teaches strategies for reaching out to the LGBT people group with Christ's love and forgiveness.

To learn more or to invite Michelle to speak visit:

WWW.PRODIGALPURSUED.COM

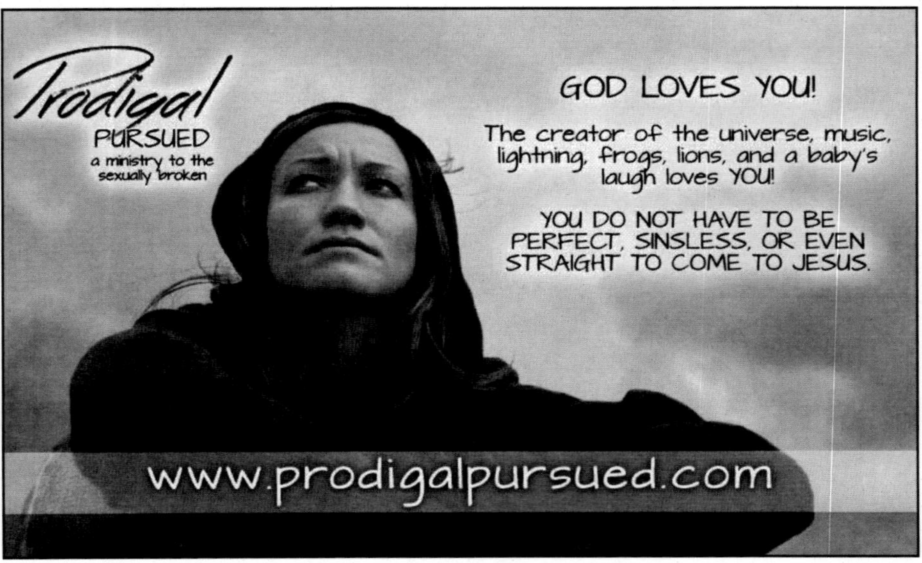